QUOTES

Every Man Should Know

QUOTES

Every Man Should Know

Edited by Nick Mamatas

QUIRK BOOKS

PHILADELPHIA

Library of Congress Cataloging in Publication Number: 2012953945

ISBN: 978-1-59474-636-9

Printed in China

Typeset in Goudy and Monotype Old Style

Designed by Katie Hatz
Production management by John J. McGurk

Quirk Books
215 Church Street
Philadelphia, PA 19106
quirkbooks.com

10 9 8 7 6 5 4 3

I wish the first word I ever said was the word "quote," so right before I die I could say "unquote."

—Steven Wright, American comedian

Introduction

"The thing about quotes from the Internet is that it's hard to verify their authenticity."

—Abraham Lincoln, U.S. president, collected on the Internet circa 2012

Why does the world need another book of quotations, especially ones every man should know? True, there are boatloads of quote books out there already. Not to mention websites and social media. Twitter is essentially a crowdsourced aphorism-generating machine, and your Facebook news feed probably gets plastered over on a daily basis by quotations with visual accompaniment (usually some kind of cat). We are all drowning in a sea of quotations, our lungs too full of wisdom to even breathe.

> "We are all drowning in a sea of quotations, our lungs too full of wisdom to even breathe."

—Nick Mamatas, American writer

Damn, there's another one.

The endless lists of quotations, the tweets, the Facebook memes—all of these are why this book is necessary. Because what guy has time to sift through that sea of mud, searching for the shiniest pearls of pithy insight? Who wants to wade elbow-deep through useless clichés about cats, sunsets, and chocolate to find time-tested words of wisdom about stuff guys value, like bravery, success, and donuts? Who's going to make sure that these quotations were actually said by the people they're said to be said by, sparing you the embarrassment of some poindexter questioning the historical accuracy of Lincoln referencing the Internet?

This guy, that's who. (You can't see me, but my thumbs are pointing at my face.)

What we hope to accomplish in this little volume is provide a selection of the best quotations from the world over and time immemorial. There are quotes you can bust out at a cocktail party to seem intelligent, quotes you can drop on the head of some fool who needs schoolin', quotes you can lean on to add levity to your next awkward silence, quotes you can use to convince a woman you're on her side (we're just giving you the words; the sincerity is up to you). We're even arming you with strategic quotes that you can whip out to out-quote anyone who dares to brandish a clumsy adage in your presence (because, as Voltaire famously said, "A witty saying proves nothing.")

Incidentally, that Voltaire quotation comes from *Le dîner du comte de Boulainvilliers*, and the context was a critique of the authority and ideological hold of the Catholic church in eighteenth-century France. In case it comes up at a cocktail party.

How to Use This Book: A Crash Course in Quoting Protocol

Be sparing. A little quoting goes a long way. You want to come off more "clever quipster" and less "exhaustive human database." Choose a few favorites for regular rotation, and refresh as necessary.

Be appropriate. Deploy a quote that's suited not just to the occasion but to the audience as well. Anyone from George Carlin to George W. Bush might be polarizing given the particular content of the quote and context in which it is used.

Be enlightening. Not everyone's smart enough to have this book in his back pocket, after all. Be prepared to contextualize unusual or unfamiliar quotes and leave everyone around you a little more educated than when you found them.

Be bold. A well-crafted turn of phrase can be a powerful statement, but only if you put it out there. Don't hesitate. Speak up. Or, to quote your kindergarten teacher, "use your words."

Chapter 1

Wisdom of the Ages

What do ancient sages, tribal prophets, and snippets of texts perhaps written under the influence of psychotropic mushrooms have to do with us today, in our topsy-turvy world of globalized economies and sexting with smartphones? Perhaps not much, but sometimes a quotation survives because it is apt for the human condition on a transhistorical, transcultural level. (Though to be honest, sometimes a quotation survives because it's so utterly ambiguous that it can be used arbitrarily in virtually any situation.) The philosophers of the past struggled with many of the same questions we face today. What does it mean to be human? What sort of life is "the good life"? What is man's relationship to the state? How can I justify boozing it up occasionally or taking frequent naps?

A store of quotations from the ancient world can be useful in any number of scenarios: boardroom discussions with your boss, heart-to-heart talks with your kid, verbal tussles with that friend of a friend who thinks he's so damn clever. Don't hesitate to draw these big guns when you need to shoot your way out of a rhetorical corner. For as Aristotle said in his

Rhetoric: "It is absurd to hold that a man ought to be ashamed of being unable to defend himself with his limbs, but not of being unable to defend himself with speech and reason, when the use of reason is more distinctive of a human being than the use of his limbs." (Warning: Not all ancient quotations are as easy to memorize as that one.)

Ancient Greece

The Greeks were cultural innovators; they created many things we still use today, such as democracy, philosophy, toast, and the vending machine. (No kidding—the Greeks had a coin-operated vending machine in the first century BC.) They weren't the first to struggle with what it means to be human, but their ideas were rigorous enough to last the test of three thousand years of Western civilization. And now, you can fake your way through a conversation about them with these nuggets of wisdom.

The unexamined life is not worth living for a human being.

>—Socrates, Greek philosopher,
>quoted in Plato's *Apology*

By means of beauty all beautiful things become beautiful.

>—Socrates, Greek philosopher,
>quoted in Plato's *Phædo*

There is only one good, knowledge, and one evil, ignorance.

>—Socrates, Greek philosopher,
>quoted in Diogenes Laertius's *Lives of Eminent Philosophers*

No pleasure is a bad thing in itself, but the things which produce certain pleasures entail disturbances many times greater than the pleasures themselves.

—Epicurus, Greek philosopher,
in *Principal Doctrines*

Even sleepers are workers and collaborators on what goes on in the universe.

—Heraclitus, Greek philosopher,
in Fragment 90

To be sure, man's life is a business which does not deserve to be taken too seriously; yet we cannot help being in earnest with it, and there's the pity.

—Plato, Greek philosopher,
in *Laws* VII 803a–b

Power is a near neighbor to necessity.
>   —Pythagoras, Greek mathematician and
>   philosopher, in *The Golden Verses*

(Pythagoras is better known among geometry students
for his most famous quote, "A squared plus B squared
equals C squared.")

Even sleepers are workers and collaborators on what
goes on in the universe.
>   —Heraclitus, Greek philosopher,
>   in Fragment 90

A man's character is his fate.
>   —Heraclitus, Greek philosopher,
>   in Fragment 121

Anybody can become angry, that is easy; but to be angry with the right person, and to the right degree, and at the right time, for the right purpose, and in the right way, that is not within everybody's power and is not easy.

—Aristotle, Greek philosopher,
in *Nicomachean Ethics*

We have two ears and one mouth, so we should listen more than we say.

—Zeno of Citum, Greek philosopher,
quoted in Diogenes Laertius's *Lives of
Eminent Philosophers*

Some say cavalry and others claim infantry or a fleet of long oars is the supreme sight on the black earth. I say it is the one you love.

> —Sappho, Greek lyric poet, as
> translated by Willis Barnstone in
> *The Complete Poems of Sappho*

The Bible

Whether you're a believer or not, there's no getting around the fact that the Bible, with its Old and New Testaments, is the foundation for morality in the Western world and has informed literature, family relationships, and geopolitics for millennia. It is easily the most popular book on earth. In fact, if you live in the United States and aren't currently wandering through Death Valley, you are almost certainly within one mile of a copy of the Bible, and probably within a few yards of one.

But have you ever actually flipped through the thing? It's huge. We're only able to scratch the surface here, but if you get a chance, be sure to take a deeper dive. (Spoiler alert: It ends with a bang.)

These quotes come from the King James Version (KJV), considered by many to be the most beautifully written of all the translations.

———

Drink no longer water, but use a little wine for thy stomach's sake and thine often infirmities.

—1 Timothy 5:23

———

As a dog returneth to his vomit, so a fool returneth to his folly.

—Proverbs 26:11

———

Greater love has no one than this, that he lay down his life for his friends.

—John 15:13

A friend loveth at all times, and a brother is born for adversity.

—Proverbs 17:17

Hope deferred maketh the heart sick: but when the desire cometh, it is a tree of life.

—Proverbs 13:12

Wealth gotten by vanity shall be diminished: but he that gathereth by labour shall increase.

—Proverbs 13:11

He that loveth silver shall not be satisfied with silver; nor he that loveth abundance with increase.

—Ecclesiastes 5:10

A soft answer turneth away wrath: but grievous words stir up anger.

—Proverbs 15:1

———————

For what is a man profited, if he shall gain the whole world, and lose his own soul?

—Matthew 16:26

———————

There is no fear in love; but perfect love casteth out fear: because fear hath torment. He that feareth is not made perfect in love.

—1 John 4:18

(This quotation, from *first* John, is good for wedding speeches and whatnot. Please don't confuse it with John 4:18: "For thou hast had five husbands; and he whom thou now hast is not thy husband: in that saidst thou truly.")

And if a kingdom be divided against itself, that kingdom cannot stand. And if a house be divided against itself, that house cannot stand.

—Mark 3:24–25

All go unto one place; all are of the dust, and all turn to dust again.

—Ecclesiastes 3:20

Ancient Rome

From poets to statesmen to philosophers, all citizens of the Roman Empire loved a good turn of phrase. These days, unless you're a doctor, lawyer, or pope, people might find it pretentious to hear you pepper your speech with Latinate non sequiturs. In English, though, these phrases add extra heft to lightweight conversations.

Men willingly believe what they wish.
—Julius Caesar, Roman dictator

Good fortune and a good disposition are rarely given to the same man.
—Livy, Roman historian

The wise man will live as long as he ought, not as long as he can.
—Seneca the Younger, Roman philosopher and statesman

Fortune favors the brave.
—Virgil, Roman poet

We must not say that every mistake is a foolish one.
—Cicero, Roman orator

For the fame of riches and beauty is fickle and frail, while virtue is eternally excellent.
—Sallust, Roman statesman and historian

The best ideas are common property.
—Seneca the Younger, Roman philosopher and statesman

Ancient China

There used to be a lot of racist jokes and aphorisms starting with the words "Confucius say . . . ," which fortunately have fallen out of favor. Still, the wisdom of Chinese sages and philosophers should not be ignored.

The superior man does not, even for the space of a single meal, act contrary to virtue. In moments of haste, he cleaves to it. In seasons of danger, he cleaves to it.

Fine words and an insinuating appearance are seldom associated with virtue.

> —Confucius, Chinese teacher and
> philosopher, in *The Analects*

The feeling of commiseration is the beginning of humanity.

> —Mencius, aka Meng Ke or Meng Ko,
> Chinese philosopher

Mastering others is strength.
Mastering yourself is true power.

—Lao Tzu, Chinese philosopher and
Taoist, in *Tao Te Ching*

Lao Tzu, also known as Laozi, is a central figure in Chinese culture. He's the author of the *Tao Te Ching* and the founder of the Chinese philsophy of Taoism, and in certain circles he has been revered as a deity. In some ways, his point of view is opposite that of Confucius, who was trying to reinforce the social order with a bajillion laws that delineated everybody's duties to everyone else. The Taoists believed that interfering with the natural order of things by imposing human constraints would be a waste of time at best, ruinous at worst.

For our purposes, the important thing to know about Lao Tzu is that his venerated book is the go-to source for enigmatic quotes with that "Tell me the secret of your kung fu, sensei" feeling. Following are some more examples.

- A journey of a thousand miles starts with a single step.

- He who knows does not speak; he who speaks does not know.

- The nameless is the beginning of heaven and earth.

- It is the empty space which makes the room useful.

- A leader is best when people barely know that he exists.

- A good traveler has no fixed plans and is not intent upon arriving.

- He who knows that enough is enough will always have enough.

- The world is won by those who let it go.

A dog is not considered a good dog because he is a good barker. A man is not considered a good man because he is a good talker.

—Zhuang Zhou, Chinese philosopher

The tongue like a sharp knife . . . kills without drawing blood.

—Traditional Chinese proverb, which has been attributed occasionally to Confucius and, more recently, the Buddha

Buddhism

Gautama Buddha, "the awakened one," was born into a wealthy family on the Indian subcontinent and rejected a life of riches and power in his search for wisdom. The religion of which he is the central figure is one of the largest in the world, and he is one of the most quotable religious figures. Indeed, the Buddha has become so trendy that many of the quotes attributed to him on T-shirts and coffee mugs and websites are not Buddhist at all. Here are a few bona fide quotations that won't add to your karmic load.

———

A fool associating himself with a wise man all his life sees not the truth, even as the spoon enjoys not the taste of the soup.

> —The Buddha, in *The Dhammapada*,
> verse 64

———

Happily the peaceful live, discarding both victory and defeat.

> —The Buddha, in *The Dhammapada*,
> verse 201

To support mother and father, to cherish wife and children, and to be engaged in peaceful occupation; this is the greatest blessing.

>—The Buddha, in *Mangala Sutta*

Some do not understand that we must die, but those who do realize this settle their quarrels.

>—The Buddha, in *The Dhammapada*,
>verse 6

Neither fire, nor moisture, nor wind can destroy the blessing of a good deed, and it will reform the whole world.

>—The Buddha, as translated by Paul Carus
>in *Gospel of the Buddha*

There is no noble truth, there is only void.
>   —Bodhidharma, Buddhist monk and
>   teacher, quoted in *Anthology of the
>   Patriarchal Hall*

Drop by drop is the water pot filled. Likewise, the fool, gathering it little by little, fills himself with evil.
>   —The Buddha, in *The Dhammapada*,
>   verse 121

Islam

With more than a billion adherents, Islam is arguably the world's largest religion. Founded only about 1,400 years ago, perhaps it doesn't qualify as ancient, but Islam's connection to the older Abrahamic religions of Judaism and Christianity qualifies it for this chapter. Founded by the prophet Mohammed after he received a revelation from God, Islam is associated with many holy books. The most important of these is the Quran, which is supplemented by the *hadiths*—sayings or actions that are attributed to Mohammed but do not appear in the Quran itself. During the eighth and ninth centuries, the hadiths were gathered into collections, such as *Sahih al-Bukhari* compiled by Muhammad al-Bukhari. Different denominations of Islam draw on different hadith collections. Here's a selection of hadiths.

Allah will not be merciful to those who are not merciful to people.

—*Sahih al-Bukhari*

It is better for a leader to make a mistake in forgiving than to make a mistake in punishing.

—*Jami al-Tirmidhi*

It is better for any of you to carry a load of firewood on his own back than begging from someone else.

—*Riyadh-Us-Saleheen*

He who takes back his present is like him who swallows his vomit.

—*Sahih al-Bukhari*

Chapter 2

Inspiration
and Action

When asked by a journalist what his message was, pacifist Indian leader Mohandas Karamchand Gandhi is reported to have said, "My life is my message." That's a statement most guys can get behind: we don't want to spend the whole day yakkin'. We want to get going already, we want to *act*, we want to *do stuff*. There's a time for words, and a time for action . . . and a time for words that spur you to action. So in this section we've curated some powerful quotations that you can use to jolt yourself or your fellows into changing the world (or coming to a consensus on where to go for lunch).

———————

I submit to you that if a man hasn't discovered something he will die for, he isn't fit to live.

—Martin Luther King Jr., American minister and civil rights activist

Wars may be fought with weapons, but they are won by men.

—George S. Patton, U.S. general

If there is effort, there is always accomplishment.

—Jigoro Kano, founder of judo

He who rejects change is the architect of decay. The only human institution which rejects progress is the cemetery.

—Harold Wilson, prime minister of the United Kingdom

I am still encouraged to go on. I wouldn't know where else to go.

—E. B. White, American writer

Whenever anything is being accomplished, it is being done, I have learned, by a monomaniac with a mission.

>—Peter Drucker, American
>management consultant

If you want to make enemies, try to change something.
>—Woodrow Wilson, U.S. president

It is not enough to have a good mind. The main thing is to use it well.

>—René Descartes, French philosopher, in
>*Discourse on Method*

There can be no great accomplishment without risk.
>—Neil Armstrong, American astronaut

I've missed more than 9,000 shots in my career. I've lost almost 300 games. Twenty-six times, I've been trusted to take the game winning shot and missed. I've failed over and over and over again in my life. And that is why I succeed.

—Michael Jordan, American professional basketball player

If you don't know the guy on the other side of the world, love him anyway because he's just like you. He has the same dreams, the same hopes and fears. It's one world, pal. We're all neighbors.

—Frank Sinatra, American singer

Risks must be taken because the greatest hazard in life is to risk nothing.

—Leo Buscaglia, American writer and motivational speaker

Use only that which works, and take it from any place you can find it.

—Bruce Lee, American martial artist

Neither a wise man nor a brave man lies down on the tracks of history to wait for the train of the future to run over him.

—Dwight D. Eisenhower, U.S. general
and president

Because things are the way they are, things will not stay the way they are.

—Bertolt Brecht, German dramatist
and poet

Take it easy, but take it.

—Woody Guthrie, American singer-songwriter

Peace cannot be kept by force. It can only be achieved by understanding.

> —Albert Einstein, German physicist

It is not enough to be industrious; so are the ants. What are you industrious about?

> —Henry David Thoreau, American writer and philosopher

If there is no struggle, there is no progress.

> —Frederick Douglass, African American abolitionist

To live is the rarest thing in the world. Most people exist, that is all.

> —Oscar Wilde, Irish writer, in *The Soul of Man Under Socialism*

I keep on making what I can't do yet in order to learn to be able to do it.

—Vincent van Gogh, Dutch painter

If you want to make an apple pie from scratch, you must first create the universe.

—Carl Sagan, American astronomer

Remember, today is the tomorrow you worried about yesterday.

—Dale Carnegie, American writer, in *How to Stop Worrying and Start Living*

Many of life's failures are people who did not realize how close they were to success when they gave up.

—Thomas Edison, American inventor

Screw it, let's do it.

—Sir Richard Branson, founder of the
Virgin Group of businesses

As far as mottos go, "Screw it, let's do it" doesn't have what you'd call gravitas. But for Branson, it works. Not only is it the title of his inspirational book, the phrase really does appear to be his guiding life principle. Branson launched a magazine called *Student* as a teenager and soon began selling records, first in a church basement and then in a London shop. Twelve years later, he founded Virgin Atlantic Airways, and his record stores quickly grew into the worldwide Virgin Megastore chain—where one could buy Virgin records, peruse books under the Virgin imprint, and guzzle Virgin Cola. In 1999, Branson launched Virgin Mobile, and in 2004 he started Virgin Galactic, to develop space travel, and Virgin Fuels, which invests in renewable energy sources. Along with all those business ventures, Branson has endeavored to break a variety of world records, such as the one for crossing the English Channel in an amphibious craft and for circumnavigating the globe via hot-air balloon.

Don't pray when it rains if you don't pray when the sun shines.

>—Satchel Paige, American Negro leagues
>and Major League Baseball pitcher

A person needs a little madness, or else they never dare cut the rope and be free.

>—Nikos Kazantzakis, Greek author
>and philosopher

When a man is denied the right to live the life he believes in, he has no choice but to become an outlaw.

>—Nelson Mandela, South African activist
>and politician, in *Long Walk to Freedom*

It's better to die upon your feet than to live upon your knees!

> —Emiliano Zapata, Mexican rebel

Cynicism masquerades as wisdom, but it is the farthest thing from it.

> —Stephen Colbert, American satirist

Fill your hands, you son of a bitch!

> —John Wayne, American film actor, as
> Rooster Cogburn in *True Grit*

(With a few important exceptions, I've avoided quoting fictional characters in this book. But damn if this isn't the perfect thing to exclaim the next time you challenge a buddy to something trivial and competitive, like a game of darts or a drinking contest.)

Chapter 3

Politics

Mark Twain once wrote, "Reader, suppose you were an idiot. And suppose you were a member of Congress. But I repeat myself." That pretty well covers most people's attitudes toward politics. But despite that widespread agreement, political discussions can get quite heated. Which is where you come in, with the perfect quote that can douse the flames in a shower of humor and eloquence. Or, if you prefer, turn up the heat by making a mockery of someone's closely held beliefs. Following are some quotations that can be applied to political situations of all types, from school-board elections to the precarious dream of world peace. If the conversation turns ugly, fall back on another quotable Twain phrase: In *What Is Man?* one of Twain's characters comments, "Fleas can be taught nearly anything that a Congressman can." Nothing unites disagreeing Americans as quickly as our dislike of representatives in Washington.

You can't lead the people if you don't love the people. You can't save the people if you won't serve the people.

—Cornel West, American author, activist, and professor

In politics an absurdity is not a handicap.

—Napoleon Bonaparte, French military leader

Every Communist must grasp the truth: political power grows out of the barrel of a gun.

—Mao Tse-Tung, Chinese communist revolutionary, in *Quotations from Chairman Mao Tse-Tung* (aka "The Little Red Book")

Society is produced by our wants, and government by wickedness.

—Thomas Paine, American political writer, in *Common Sense*

A conquering army on the border will not be stopped by eloquence.

—Otto von Bismarck, first chancellor of Germany

They who can give up essential liberty to obtain a little temporary safety, deserve neither liberty nor safety.

—Benjamin Franklin, founding father of the United States

If men were angels, no government would be necessary. If angels were to govern men, neither external nor internal controls on government would be necessary.

—James Madison, U.S. president

As I would not be a slave, so I would not be a master. This expresses my idea of democracy.

—Abraham Lincoln, U.S. president

Man is by nature a political animal.

—Aristotle, Greek philosopher, in *Politics*

Those who make peaceful revolution impossible will make violent revolution inevitable.

—John F. Kennedy, U.S. president

A country cannot subsist well without liberty, nor liberty without virtue.

—Jean-Jacques Rousseau, French philosopher

Dictators ride to and fro on tigers from which they dare not dismount. And the tigers are getting hungry.

—Winston Churchill, prime minister of the United Kingdom

The legitimate powers of government extend to such acts only as are injurious to others. But it does me no injury for my neighbor to say there are twenty gods, or no god. It neither picks my pocket nor breaks my leg.

—Thomas Jefferson, U.S. president

How can you govern a country which has two hundred and forty-six varieties of cheese?
—Charles de Gaulle, French military
leader and president

It is bad policy to fear the resentment of an enemy.
—Ethan Allen, American revolutionary

The cost of liberty is less than the price of repression.
—W. E. B. Du Bois, American
civil rights activist

It only takes 20 years for a liberal to become a conservative without changing a single idea.
—Robert Anton Wilson, American writer,
in *The Illuminati Papers*

When I'm president, everyone gets a free pony.
—Vermin Supreme, 2012 U.S.
presidential candidate

A conservative is someone who believes in reform.
But not now.
—Mort Sahl, American comedian

It was amazing I won. I was running against peace
and prosperity and incumbency.
—George W. Bush, U.S. president

In politics, if you want anything said, ask a man. If
you want anything done, ask a woman.
—Margaret Thatcher, British
prime minister

Dictatorships foster oppression, dictatorships foster servitude, dictatorships foster cruelty; more abominable is the fact that they foster idiocy.
>—Jorge Luis Borges, Argentine writer

There's no trick to being a humorist when you have the whole government working for you.
>—Will Rogers, American humorist

You have to remember one thing about the will of the people: it wasn't that long ago that we were swept away by the Macarena.
>—Jon Stewart, American comedian
>and writer

History teaches that wars begin when governments believe the price of aggression is cheap.

— Ronald Reagan, U.S. president

―――――

Anyone who is capable of getting themselves made President should on no account be allowed to do the job.

— Douglas Adams, English writer, in
The Restaurant at the End of the Universe

―――――

A good politician, under democracy, is quite as unthinkable as an honest burglar.

— H. L. Mencken, American writer
and satirist

History is merely a list of surprises. It can only prepare us to be surprised yet again.

—Kurt Vonnegut, American writer,
in *Slapstick*

The first lesson a revolutionary must learn is that he is a doomed man.

—Huey P. Newton, American
political activist

The difference between a rebel and a patriot depends upon who is in power at the moment.

—Sidney Sheldon, American writer,
in *The Sands of Time*

Chapter 4

Humor

A word of warning about this chapter: few things are as unfunny as a joke retold too many times. We remember funny quotes because they were good the first time around, not because they're so awesome when you say, "As Winston Churchill once said . . ." and then stammer your way through the rest of it. So before you blurt out any of these gems, be sure you have the wording down and can deliver the quotes smoothly. Some of this chapter's selections are witticisms, clever one-liners that also say something about the world. Others are outright jokes, which you might try to work into a conversation or just blurt out as wacky non sequiturs when everyone's looking bored. Try not to fire off too many of these in a row, though. Nobody likes the guy who obviously memorized some stand-up comedy routine and decided to try it out over the punchbowl at an otherwise perfectly lovely party.

A severed foot is the ultimate stocking stuffer.
    —Mitch Hedberg, American comedian

I have never killed anyone, but I have read some obituary notices with great satisfaction.

> —Clarence Darrow, American lawyer,
> in *The Story of My Life*

I don't need you to remind me of my age, I have a bladder to do that for me.

> —Stephen Fry, English actor, in *Paperweight*

Early to rise and early to bed makes a male healthy and wealthy and dead.

> —James Thurber, American humorist

My way of joking is to tell the truth. It's the funniest joke in the world.

> —George Bernard Shaw,
> English playwright

I really didn't say everything I said. Then again, I might have said 'em, but you never know.

—Yogi Berra, American baseball player and manager

Lawrence Peter "Yogi" Berra had a nineteen-year career in major league baseball, is one of the greatest catchers in the history of the game, and appeared in twenty-one World Series championships as a player, coach, or manager. But he's best known for his "yogiisms," which are irresistibly quotable combinations of paradox and wisdom. Here are some of the most notable examples.

- Always go to other people's funerals; otherwise they won't go to yours.

- Little things are big.

- You can observe a lot by watching.

- The future ain't what it used to be.

- If you can't imitate him, don't copy him.

- If you don't know where you're going, you might not get there.

- It's déjà vu all over again.

- Ninety percent of this game is mental, and the other half is physical.

And perhaps his most famous:

It ain't over till it's over.

I believe that every erection is a miracle.
—Larry David, American comedy writer,
on *Curb Your Enthusiasm*

I like staying in hotels. I like their tiny soap. I like to pretend it's regular-sized and my muscles are huge.
—Jerry Seinfeld, American comedian

God gave men both a penis and a brain, but unfortunately not enough blood supply to run both at the same time.
—Robin Williams, American comedian

Thought: Why does man kill? He kills for food. And not only food: frequently there must be a beverage.
—Woody Allen, American writer and
humorist, in *Without Feathers*

If every word a person says has to be right and balanced and fair, I will jump off a tall thing onto a hard place.

—Louis C.K., American comedian
(via Twitter)

When confronted with anyone who holds my lack of religious faith in such contempt, I say, "It's the way God made me."

—Ricky Gervais, English actor and writer

Happiness is having a large, loving, caring, close-knit family in another city.

—George Burns, American comedian

It's great when what you want to do and what you're supposed to do are the same thing. Like when a married couple have sex with each other.

—Mario Joyner, American comedian
(via Twitter)

I wish the first word I ever said was the word "quote," so right before I die I could say "unquote."

—Steven Wright, American comedian

It's so hard to get an intervention when people don't think you have any problems.

—Maria Bamford, American comedian

All you need is ignorance and confidence; then success is sure.

—Mark Twain, American humorist

I once asked my father for a dollar for the school picnic. He told me how he once killed a grizzly bear with his loose-leaf notebook.

—Bill Cosby, American comedian
and actor

Without laughter, life on our planet would be intolerable.

—Steve Allen, American comedian
and television personality

Men can go for decades without thinking about their buttocks. A man's buttocks could have moss growing on them (I have seen this) and he would not necessarily be aware of it.

—Dave Barry, American humorist

If your enemy is laughing, how can he bludgeon you to death?
>—Mel Brooks, American screenwriter
>and film director

Follow seven beers with a couple of scotches and a thimble of good marijuana, and it's funny how sleep just sort of comes on its own.
>—David Sedaris, American writer

It takes a big man to cry, but it takes a bigger man to laugh at that man.
>—Jack Handey, American humorist,
>in *Deep Thoughts*

What's the use of happiness? It can't buy you money.
—Henny Youngman, British
American comedian

I once saw my grandparents having sex, and that's why I don't eat raisins.
—Zach Galifianakis, American
comedian and actor

Nothing, believe me, nothing is more satisfying to me personally than getting a great idea and then beatin' it to death.
—David Letterman, American
television talk-show host

Chapter 5

Women

Wherever two men gather, there will be, eventually, some talk about women. And most of the commentary falls into two categories: "Women be crazy" and "Damn, that is one fine woman." A disconcertingly large proportion of quotes about women—by men, at least—fall into the first category. It could be that highlighting the differences between the sexes is inherently more interesting. But it also seems that guys tend to reserve their unabashed praise for *specific* women in their lives, their mothers and lovers and the ones who got away, while venting their gender-based criticisms and frustrations on womanhood as a whole. As great as any one particular woman we know might be, we seem to have a hard time believing that there are more of them out there.

Women are a beautiful complication, and I look forward to far more beauties and far more complications.
    —Keith Richards, English rock guitarist

Woman must not depend upon the protection of man, but must be taught to protect herself.

  —Susan B. Anthony, American suffragette

You ever hear girls say, "I'm not religious, but I'm spiritual"? I like to reply with "I'm not honest, but you're interesting!"

  —Daniel Tosh, American comedian

No one but a woman in love ever sees the maximum of men's greatness.

  —Anaïs Nin, American author

I'd much rather be a woman than a man. Women can cry, they can wear cute clothes, and they are the first to be rescued off of sinking ships.

  —Gilda Radner, American actress

To keep your marriage brimming,
With love in the loving cup,
Whenever you're wrong, admit it;
Whenever you're right, shut up.
—Ogden Nash, American poet
and humorist

For any relationship to work, both people have to be on the same page, both people have to have the same focus, and we all know what that page is. We all know what that focus is. In order for the relationship to work both people have to have the same focus, and what's that focus? That focus is all about *her*!
—Chris Rock, American comedian

A lady is one who never shows her underwear unintentionally.
—Lillian Day, American author

Buying my wife a gun is sorta like me saying "Y'know, I kinda wanna kill myself . . . but I want it to be a surprise."

> —Marc Maron, American comedian and
> radio and podcast host

Women have two orgasms, the real ones and the ones they make up on their own. And I can give you the male point of view on this, which is: we're fine with it. You do whatever you have to do, and we'll do whatever we have to.

> —Jerry Seinfeld, American comedian

As usual, there is a great woman behind every idiot.

> —John Lennon, English musician
> and activist

I remember after I got that marriage license I went across from the license bureau to a bar for a drink. The bartender said, "What will you have, sir?" And I said, "A glass of hemlock."

—Ernest Hemingway, American writer

For me there are only two kinds of women, goddesses and doormats.

—Pablo Picasso, Spanish painter

Well-behaved women seldom make history.

—Laurel Thatcher Ulrich,
American historian

If you can make a girl laugh, you can make her do anything.

—Marilyn Monroe, American actress

Women are crazy, men are stupid. And the main reason women are crazy is that men are stupid.
> —George Carlin, American comedian

I like a woman with a head on her shoulders. I hate necks.
> —Steve Martin, American actor,
> comedian, and writer

Every time we liberate a woman, we liberate a man.
> —Margaret Mead, American
> cultural anthropologist

Women who seek to be equal with men lack ambition.
> —Timothy Leary, American
> psychologist and writer

Woman is sacred; the woman one loves is holy.
>—Alexandre Dumas, French writer, in
>*The Count of Monte Cristo*

Kindness in women, not their beauteous looks, shall win my love.
>—William Shakespeare, English writer,
>in *The Taming of the Shrew*

Being a woman is a terribly difficult trade since it consists principally of dealings with men.
>—Joseph Conrad, Polish writer, in *Chance*

I have got little feet, because nothing grows in the shade.
>—Dolly Parton, American singer

At the age of eleven or thereabouts women acquire a poise and an ability to handle difficult situations which a man, if he is lucky, manages to achieve somewhere in the later seventies.

—P. G. Wodehouse, English writer,
in *Uneasy Money*

The great question that has never been answered, and which I have not yet been able to answer, despite my thirty years of research into the feminine soul, is "What does a woman want?"

—Sigmund Freud, Austrian neurologist
and founder of psychoanalysis

I'll promise to go easier on drinking and to get to bed earlier, but not for you, fifty thousand dollars, or two-hundred and fifty thousand dollars will I give up women. They're too much fun.

—Babe Ruth, American baseball player

Chapter 6

They Never
Said That

Let's face it: Most offices, parties, lunch tables, and other social settings have room for only one Quote Guy. And since you went to all the trouble of buying and reading this book, you want to dissuade any rivals from trying to usurp your role as King Maxim. One way to frighten off would-be challengers is to undermine their credibility. Fortunately, quotes get mangled, shortened, misattributed, and, increasingly, simply made up by anyone with a cute photo of a cat and a broadband Internet connection. Sooner or later your enemy will put forth one of these bogus quotations, and then you can respond with a crushing blow of accuracy.

Here we debunk a few of the most common misquotes.

Be the change you want to see in the world.

—Mohandas Karamchand Gandhi,
Indian pacifist leader

Close, but no hunger strike. While the sentiment behind this oft-dorm-room-posted sentence hews closely to what Gandhi professed, his actual statement on the matter was:

"If we could change ourselves, the tendencies in the world would also change. As a man changes his own nature, so does the attitude of the world change towards him. . . . We need not wait to see what others do."

But that doesn't fit so well on a T-shirt, hence the familiar paraphrase.

Be kind; everyone you meet is fighting a hard battle.

—Plato, Greek philosopher

This one doesn't even *sound* like Plato. If there was one thing Plato wasn't overly concerned with, it was the well-being of "everyone." According to Plato, nature "shows, among men as well as among animals, and indeed among whole cities and races, that justice consists in the superior ruling over and having more than the inferior."

The touchy-feely faux-Plato quote seems to have been first put in print in 1897 by a journalist at the *British Weekly*, who was delivering a Christmas message from Scottish author and clergyman Ian Macleran to the paper's readers: "Be pitiful, for every man is fighting a hard battle." At the time, the word "pitiful" was often used in the sense of being full of pity, or compassion, for others. How this warm-hearted nineteenth-century sentiment ended up in the mouth of an ancient Greek elitist is a question for the ages.

Success is not the key to happiness; happiness is the key to success.

There has to be evil, so that good can prove its purity above it.

The greatest prayer is patience.

Any quote involving "suffering," "happiness," "compassion," or "peace."

—The Buddha

In the West, probably no religious icon is credited with more dubious quotations than the Buddha. It makes sense. The Buddha was a great spiritual and moral leader, but Buddhism is a relatively recent import to the United States. There are many different Buddhist traditions, and relatively few of the texts associated with the faith have been properly translated and distributed. This means that any reasonable-sounding bit of spiritual gobbledy-gook could be attributed to the Buddha and then passed around the Internet indefinitely. Your best bet: Consider all Buddha quotes suspect until you can vet them against the excellent website FakeBuddhaQuotes.com.

Elementary, my dear Watson.

—Sherlock Holmes, detective

Sometimes used by people who want to passive-aggressively point out some obvious truth that you overlooked, this phrase evokes Sherlock Holmes gently chiding Watson for being a complete moron. Except he never said it, not in any of Arthur Conan Doyle's stories about the great detective. Who's the moron now, buddy?

The definition of "insanity" is doing the same thing over and over and expecting different results.

—Albert Einstein, German physicist

Nope. As scientific and mathematical as it may sound, this statement didn't come from Einstein, nor from Benjamin Franklin or Mark Twain, who've also been attached to it. It may have been injected into the public consciousness by mystery writer Rita Mae Brown. In any case, is it really a good idea never to try doing anything more than once? If that were the case, would we ever have made it to the top of Mount Everest, put space probes on Mars, or developed hair-care products that both clean *and* condition? What ever happened to "If at first you don't succeed, try, try again"?

God made beer because he loves us and wants us to be happy.

—Benjamin Franklin, founding father
of the United States

Oh, if only. The idea that one of our founding fathers would so ably combine religion and brewskis is so appealing that it's easy to see why this quote ends up on so many mugs and steins. Unfortunately, there's no evidence that Franklin said this, which is pretty damning given that he was a printer not shy about publishing his own words. Franklin did write something similar about wine; maybe the misquote happened because Ben seems like such a beer kind of guy. For starters, there's that beer belly, and only someone with a beer buzz would think it's a good idea to fly a kite in a thunderstorm.

That's one small step for a man, one giant leap for mankind.

—Neil Armstrong, American astronaut

We realize we're stepping onto hallowed ground here, though it's not as hazardous as the pock-marked lunar surface. So let us say right from the outset that the first human being to walk on the damn moon doesn't need earthbound pinheads criticizing his diction. That said, if you listen to the recording of Armstrong's historic words, he seems to have left out the "a," which is why many renderings of the quotation appear as "one small step for [a] man." Armstrong clearly intended to say "a man," and for years he and others believed that static had obscured the seemingly absent article. Recent analyses of the original broadcast suggest that he in fact didn't voice the "a." But let's face it, the man had other concerns at the time.

As an expression of human achievement that transcended nationalism and the rivalry of the space race, Armstrong's poetic phrase has a meaning that was lost on no one. The couplet does seems to have originated with Armstrong himself, not in the NASA public relations department, though it's not clear if he composed it before the

Apollo mission. You might think that Armstrong, who left our planet forever in 2012, would be quick to claim authorship of the first words spoken by a human being on extraterrestrial soil. But that wasn't his style. Armstrong tended to stay out of the public eye after resigning from NASA, and he gave few interviews. When you've spoken to the world from the surface of the moon, what else is there to say?

Chapter 7

Reviving
Clichéd Quotes

Some quotations take the form of proverbs or sayings. It hardly matters who first coined them; what's important is the wisdom they contain. Aphorisms are bits of cognitive shorthand, a way to navigate life while keeping in mind the collective knowledge of previous generations. But that doesn't mean you can't use them to show how clever and erudite you are. The next time someone bores everyone present with one of these hoary chestnuts, blow the dust off the conversation by delving into the meaning behind the clichés.

The road to hell is paved with good intentions.

This phrase seems to come from Saint Bernard of Clairvaux, who declared, "Hell is full of good wishes and desires." Basically, the phrase means that intentions are insufficient and could even lead to bad actions and thus terrible ends. The ends don't necessarily justify the means, and indeed bad means may lead to bad ends anyway. A desire to do good can lead to disaster, if the desire overwhelms common sense and ethics.

A stitch in time saves nine.

Most of us don't do much stitching in a typical day, surgeons excepted. But back in the old days, people used to mend their torn clothes rather than tossing them in the trash and buying something new and cheap (thanks, sweatshop laborers on the other side of the planet). The best strategy for mending a piece of clothing is to stitch a hole as soon as it appears. One stitch done properly and right away will keep the hole from getting larger, which could require having to do even more stitching later on. Clearly, we have evolved past this whole stitching-our-own-clothes business, but the idea of performing a little necessary work in a timely manner to avoid even more work in the future remains a good thing to keep in mind. It also sounds better than "Preventative maintenance is a rational and cost-effective action."

There's more than one way to skin a cat.

Some people claim that this aphorism—which simply means that there is more than one way to perform some important task effectively—refers either to catfish, which do often require skinning before cooking, or to the gymnastic move called skinning a cat. But, sad to say, animal slaughter has a long history in aphorisms. One early version of this saying is "There are more ways to kill a dog than hanging," which is from seventeenth-century Britain. This early version actually has a slightly different connotation—there are more ways to perform an evil act than the most obvious.

Cats took over this saying in the nineteenth century. In the 1855 novel *Westward Ho!* by Charles Kingsley, one character exclaims that there are "more ways of killing a cat than choking her with cream." There too we see a slightly different connotation from that of the original—there are more ways to accomplish a goal than through doing what someone else wants. By the time of Mark Twain's 1889 novel,

A Connecticut Yankee in King Arthur's Court, we have the modern version of the phrase: "She was wise, subtle, and knew more than one way to skin a cat." Yikes! Do we even have to skin the cat at all? Here's an alternative for the ailurophiles out there: There are more ways to the woods than one.

Early to bed and early to rise, makes a man healthy, wealthy, and wise.

This one is supposedly from Benjamin Franklin, though the notion is far more ancient. In *The Treatyse of Fysshynge with an Angle*, a book on angling published in 1496, we are told, "As the old English proverb says: 'Whoever will rise early shall be holy, healthy, and happy.'" In other words, it was already an old saying several centuries before Franklin and his almanac.

Is this quotation accurate? Well, it probably was, before industrial society and electric light. In an agricultural society, getting up early to do work and thus taking advantage of every moment of daylight was undoubtedly a good idea. Going to bed early, rather than spending one's evenings in pubs and whorehouses, was probably a better recipe for health than the alternatives and kept sinning to an unfortunate minimum as well. But in these days of science? Twentieth-century humorist James Thurber declared that early rising and early sleep makes us "healthy, wealthy, and dead." And he had electric lights and such, so he'd know. So which is it?

In 2006, Kenneth J. Mukamal, Gregory A. Wellenius, and Murray A. Mittleman performed a study on heart patients to find out if early rising and early sleeping make them healthier, wealthier, or wiser. (Wisdom being hard to quantify, the researchers swapped educational attainment for wisdom.) Shockingly, the study "found no evidence to support the Franklin or Thurber hypotheses that sleep habits dictate health, wealth or wisdom, either for the good or the bad."

So go ahead and keep whatever hours you like. And if someone questions you, here's the citation to send them: "Early to bed and early to rise: Does it matter?" (*Canadian Medical Association Journal* 175, issue 12 [December 5, 2006], pp 1560–62).

A bird in the hand is worth two in the bush.

This classic line comes from medieval Latin, though it originally ended with "in the woods" rather than "in the bush." More poetic is the similar aphorism by Ahiqar, the Assyrian sage from the sixth century BC, which can be found in his *Proverbs*: "A sparrow in the hand is worth a thousand sparrows flying." However, the whole of the capitalist economy would suggest that this isn't true. In the modern era at least, risk equals reward. Safe investments tend to have the lowest return, and risky investments—the betting of that bird in the hand *and* the leveraging of the two in the bush in the bush-bird futures market against a potential gain of those thousand flying sparrows—well, that's how millionaires are made. Of course, that's also how fortunes are lost, and these days many birds in the hand are actually mortgaged twice over and ready to be foreclosed upon.

Laughter is the best medicine.

The sentiment is an ancient one, with perhaps the most famous version from the King James Bible: "A merry heart doeth good like a medicine: but a broken spirit drieth the bones." (Proverbs, 17:22). Of course, that version doesn't say that laughter is the *best* medicine. If you have syphilis, for example, penicillin is probably the better medicine for you. But laughter is still good for you. In a not very funny article in the journal of the Federation of American Societies for Experimental Biology entitled "Cortisol and Catecholamine Stress Hormone Decrease Is Associated with the Behavior of Perceptual Anticipation of Mirthful Laughter," researchers Lee Berk, Stanley A. Tan, and Dottie Berk reported that laughing reduced levels of cortisol and other stress hormones while increasing beta-endorphins and human growth hormone. Indeed, even anticipating a good laugh had a positive effect on the study subjects' hormone levels.

Like father, like son.

This little proverb has an ancient provenance and can be found in both the West and Asia. It used to be wordier, as in Alexander Barclay's 1509 poem "The Ship of Fools" (which itself was partially a translation of a German text by Sebastian Brant): "An olde prouerbe hath longe agone be sayde That oft the sone in maners lyke wyll be Vnto the Father."

The English language was crazy back then. What's more, even in the sixteenth century, this saying was considered old. Still, in 1709 Oswald Dyke had to explain the old saw, a bit, in his *British Proverbs with Moral Reflexions*: "Like Father, like Son. How many Sons inherit their Fathers Failings, as well as Estates?" Lots of them, Mr. Dyke, lots of them.

The truth of the proverb is self-evident. For a long time, modern psychology and biology have been preoccupied with the question of nature versus nurture: Is one's behavior determined by genes or by how the person was raised? Either way, because most parents raise their own children, "like father, like son" rings true. No wonder it seems to be so common a claim. And although "like father, like daughter" and "like parent, like child" are just as true, the proverb seems most often phrased to explain a son's negative behavior. Perhaps its longevity is due to mothers occasionally wishing to throw up their hands rather than blame their own genetic or behavioral influences on their child. Honestly, who can blame them?

Let sleeping dogs lie.

This proverb simply means that one shouldn't restart old arguments or controversies, even if they've not been settled, as long as they're not currently active. Let the matter rest. Originally, the proverb was conceptualized slightly differently. Chaucer had it as "It is nought good a slepyng hound to wake" in his 1380 poem *Troilus and Criseyde*. The meaning doesn't change overmuch by altering the advice, and "let sleeping dogs lie" is more euphonious than the older version, although Chaucer's formulation did last for a couple of centuries. By the nineteenth century, the modern version was common enough, and it can be found in Charles Dickens's *David Copperfield*: "Let sleeping dogs lie. Who wants to rouse 'em?" says Uriah Heep, who nevertheless is the antagonist of the book. Sometimes a sleeping dog does need a good poke, if only to generate an interesting story.

Chapter 8

Quote vs.

Counterquote

We could not wholly confirm the provenance of the following quotation, so be sure to recite it with a shrug and a waggle of the hand. But the philosopher George Santayana has been cited as having said, "Almost every wise saying has an opposite one, no less wise, to balance it." Whether he ever said this or not, he's clearly correct. Sayings, quotations, and aphorisms are heuristics for the human brain to navigate the world, but it must be understood that the world is very large and human brains are very small. The guidance that quotations give us can never be universal—there are simply too many possibilities out there for One Great Quotation to lead us all. Indeed, were there One Great Quotation, you wouldn't need a book like this one. You can, however, turn this situation to your advantage by always being ready with a counterquote should someone dare to fire one of these familiar wisdom bullets in your direction.

They say: "Two wrongs don't make a right."

You say: "Turnabout is fair play."

Ah, which old saying is superior? This is actually an important political question, especially when it comes to international affairs. Nations, ethnic groups, and other parties in conflict often trade atrocities. At worst, this dynamic can spiral into endless bloodshed and feuding, leading to misery for all. Still, who are we to say that an oppressed minority cannot fight back against its oppressor? Is self-defense the same as murder? Is retribution the same as self-defense? Do the bloody means sometimes justify the peaceful ends? And you thought two wrongs not making a right was only about how you shouldn't have pulled your older sister's hair after she smacked you that one time. In fact, "two wrongs don't make a right" is an ethical warning against doing wrong regardless of the circumstances. But what is really needed in the world today is a practical warning against doing wrong. That is, we need to warn the other fellow, not our own selves, not to do wrong. May we recommend: "Don't start none, won't be none."

They say: "Absence makes the heart grow fonder."

You say: "Out of sight, out of mind."

Here, the dueling aphorisms seem to be in conflict with each other, but in fact neither is universally applicable and the two ideas are quite complementary. Absence makes the heart grow fonder when the heart is already fond, that is, when a relationship is on the upswing, when infatuation turns to love and a person's flaws drop away. Our beloved hometowns, the cherished foods of our childhoods, that favorite book from high school all seem so much better than they really are, because we started out with some affection for them. And that's what you remember when the object of your affection isn't in your face.

Similarly, out of sight becomes out of mind when that affection has started to fade or when it was never there in the first place. When you're already tired of your romantic partner, when you grew up in a boring suburb, when the foods you ate as a kid were off-brand confections from the discount store. Can you ever forget your first bite of a Li'l Deebie's Donut Twig? We already have.

They say: "Don't look a gift horse in the mouth."

You say: "Beware of Greeks bearing gifts."

Had the Trojans looked their gift horse in the mouth, they might have seen a squad of well-muscled Greeks armed to the teeth, but the first aphorism isn't about Homer's *Odyssey*. Someone familiar with equines can tell a lot about the general health and age of a horse by looking into its mouth and examining the teeth. But that would be rude if the horse was a present, tantamount to questioning the animal's value. So the proverb is a simple one: just accept the gift graciously.

Unless the gift is given by an army of Greek warriors. In modern parlance, there is no ethnic slur meant by this saying. The "Greek" in question is anyone offering a suspiciously timed present. In *The Odyssey*, the Greeks spent a decade at the walls of Troy and then suddenly sailed away, leaving behind the wooden horse as tribute. Sounds kinda suspicious, doesn't it? The horse was a symbol of Troy, but still it was very strange. (A similar trick would be attempted, unsuccessfully, by Arthur and his knights in the movie *Monty Python and the Holy Grail*.) It was Virgil who first coined the phrase "*Timeo Danaos et dona ferentes*" ("I fear Greeks, even those bearing gifts") in his epic poem *The Aeneid*. Laocoön, a Trojan priest, warns his countrymen of the guile of Odysseus and the very obvious trick that the wooden horse must be. Luckily for my Greek ancestors, nobody listened to Laocoön.

We feel compelled to point out that conspicuous generosity is a major part of Greek culture, so if you receive a present from a Greek, you're probably going to enjoy it greatly and not be slaughtered by sword-wielding soldiers. Greeks have their own version of the gift-horse proverb, but it involves a donkey. So beware of Greeks who don't like gift donkeys.

They say: "There are no stupid questions."

You say: "It is better to remain silent and be thought a fool than to open one's mouth and remove all doubt."

You know what? There actually are stupid questions. For example, the question asked moments after the answer has already been made clear. And the question that makes it obvious that the person asking it has no idea what the conversation is about. And any question that begins, "Did you see that picture on Facebook that . . ." At the very least, we can all agree that the modern variation on the aphorism—there are no stupid questions, but there are a whole lot of inquisitive idiots—holds true.

Silence, on the other hand, and as the old saying goes, is golden. It's the easiest thing in the world not to say anything. But silence comes with its own dangers, like silently assuming that your current assumptions and suppositions are correct. So when do you ask a question and risk seeming like an idiot? Since silence can always be broken but a question can never be . . . uh . . . unasked, often the best course is to hold on to the query that's potentially boneheaded, make sure you can't find the answer on the Googlenet, and ask it in a more private setting. More important is to remember that, yes, there *are* stupid questions, and if you've never asked one, you probably don't ask enough questions.

They say: "Silence is golden."

You say: "The squeaky wheel gets the grease."

Okay, silence is golden, and suffering in silence can even be admirable. But it's equally true that complaining is important—few things motivate a change of the status quo like complaints, whether it's a demand to talk to the manager at a fast food restaurant or street protests featuring thousands of angry people with picket signs and/or Molotov cocktails. For this duel, the answer to the question of whether silence is golden depends on who is doing the asking. In the case of the incompetent manager or the corrupt political regime, silence is clearly golden, and sometimes it's literally golden, too, so long as it's the silence of other people in the face of profit. To put it another way: Is your silence putting gold in their pockets?

They say: "Knowledge is power."

You say: "Ignorance is bliss."

The "Ignorance is bliss" proverb is not actually recommending ignorance as a lifestyle choice in order to achieve a state of bliss. The phrase comes from the poem "Ode on a Distant Prospect of Eton College" by Thomas Gray. The text, which is both a paean to education and an ode to lost innocence, ends, "where ignorance is bliss, / 'Tis folly to be wise." The narrator is a graduate of that famed college—a preparatory school for teens, in the British idiom—musing while looking down onto the campus at the young schoolboys living lives of ignorant bliss. As a graduate who has gone off into the world, he encountered "black Misfortune's baleful train" and is envious of the twerps playing their games on the grassy grounds.

However, ignorance doesn't guarantee bliss, especially when you're expected to be a grown-up. Terrors are visited unto the ignorant all the time, most often by the powerful. Sadly, knowledge doesn't always equal power, either. But to the extent that knowledge does imply some level of responsibility, which in turn implies a level of authority, then we can best understand these two old sayings as representing a continuum—ignorance is bliss, and knowledge eliminates that bliss but can also lead to power, which isn't necessarily all it's cracked up to be. Indeed, another famous quotation, this one from Shakespeare's *Henry VI, Part II*, comes to mind: "Uneasy lies the head that wears a crown" (act III, scene 1).

And you probably thought the quotation was "Heavy is the head that wears the crown." See, now you're becoming more knowledgeable and a teensy bit more powerful.

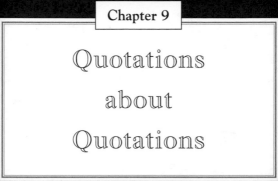

Chapter 9

Quotations
about
Quotations

Quotations can be incredibly useful for speeches, casual conversations, the formulation of life advice, and the engraving of monument cornerstones. Quotations can also be incredibly annoying, wrongheaded, outmoded, reactionary, and just plain ol' stupid. Eventually, you might encounter someone who knows nothing about anything but who does have a pocketful of quotations for any occasion. If you can't catch that guy in a misattributed quote (see "They Never Said That"), overshadow him by explaining his lame clichés (see "Reviving Clichéd Quotes"), or counter his quote with one of your own (see "Quote vs. Counterquote"), there's one more option for preserving your own Quote Guy crown. You can go nuclear with a quote that calls into question the very value of the quotation itself. Surely, as you've already figured out, there is something anachronistic about the idea of aphorisms or maxims. "Contemporary culture isn't stately enough, or stable enough, to support them," as literary critic Anatole Broyard once said in the pages of the *New York Times*.

When the sum of all human knowledge (and

cat pictures) is just a few mouse clicks away, is there really any value to memorizing the words of some bygone pontificator? We would argue that there is, but raising the question could throw your quotin' competitor off balance. Keep these anti-quote quotes handy, but use them at your own risk. Once you've admitted that quotations aren't all they're cracked up to be, you've also disarmed yourself.

―――――

But quotations and aphorisms are generally just verbal Christmas presents; enticingly done up in pretty paper and ribbons, but once you get them open they generally turn out to be just socks.
—Tom Holt, English writer, in *Barking*

―――――

Platitudes are safe, because they're easy to wink at, but truth is something else again.
—Hunter S. Thompson, American writer
and journalist

Genuine bons mots surprise those from whose lips they fall, no less than they do those who listen to them.

—Joseph Joubert, French essayist,
in *Pensées*

It is a good thing for an uneducated man to read books of quotations.

—Winston Churchill, prime minister of the
United Kingdom

(In its original context—Churchill was discussing his early education in *My Early Life: A Roving Commission*—the statement is undeniably pro-quote. But if you bust it out after someone's dared to utter an inferior quotation in your presence, it's a fairly nasty rebuke.)

One has to secrete a jelly in which to slip quotations down people's throats, and one always secretes too much jelly.

—Virginia Woolf, English writer

A facility for quotation covers the absence of original thought.

—Dorothy L. Sayers, English writer and poet, in *Gaudy Night*

I hate quotations. Tell me what you know.

—Ralph Waldo Emerson, American poet

(Ironically, by quoting him, you'll be doing exactly what Emerson hates.)

A fine quotation is a diamond on the finger of a man of wit, and a pebble in the hand of a fool.
—Joseph Roux, French Catholic priest and poet, in *Meditations of a Parish Priest*

We have now sunk to a depth at which the restatement of the obvious is the first duty of intelligent men.
—George Orwell, English novelist and journalist

Occasionally words must serve to veil the facts.
—Niccolò Machiavelli, Italian statesman and philosopher

Quotation confesses inferiority.
—Ralph Waldo Emerson, American poet, in *Letters and Social Aims*

Beware of thinkers whose minds function only when they are fueled by a quotation.

> —Emil Cioran, Romanian writer,
> in *Anathemas and Admirations*

Nothing so absurd can be said that some philosopher had not said it.

> —Cicero, Roman orator,
> in *Concerning Divination*

In a pinch, any orphan quote can be called a Chinese proverb.

> —Ralph Keyes, American writer,
> in *"Nice Guys Finish Seventh": False Phrases,
> Spurious Sayings, and Familiar Misquotations*

The devil can cite Scripture for his purpose.
>—William Shakespeare, English writer,
>in *The Merchant of Venice*

Quotation, n. The act of repeating erroneously the words of another.
>—Ambrose Bierce, American writer and
>satirist, in *The Devil's Dictionary*

For me, there's a kind of absolute power to saying the opposite of what you feel.
>—Sarah Silverman, American comedian

(Use that one if one of your quotes doesn't go over so well.)

Shake was a dramatist of note;
He lived by writing things to quote.
—Henry Cuyler Bunner, American
novelist and poet

You don't have to know everything, but you should learn how and where to find the things you need and want to know.
—Sophonisba Breckinridge, American
educator and social activist

For a quotation is a handy thing to have about, saving one the trouble of thinking for oneself, always a laborious business.
—A. A. Milne, English author

Chapter 10

Epigraphs

An epigraph is a phrase or quotation presented at the beginning of a text for any of a number of aesthetic or political reasons. Dostoyevsky used biblical passages as epigraphs; Stephen King prefers lyrics from 1960s rock and roll and quotations from novels by better novelists than he. An epigraph can be about anything—it need not even "agree" thematically with the text that follows. As such, please find a last little grab bag of quotes that did not quite fit in the previous chapters but might be perfect for term papers and short stories, on your business card, as an e-mail signature, or for anything else you'd like to class up a bit with some catchy phraseology. Some are dramatic; others are funny. And a few make a statement that's baffling enough to impress friends and confuse your enemies. Choose wisely.

Since flesh can't stay, we pass the words along.
—Erica Jong, American writer

Every normal man must be tempted, at times, to spit upon his hands, hoist the black flag, and begin slitting throats.

—H. L. Menken, American
writer and satirist

Learning carries within itself certain dangers because out of necessity one has to learn from one's enemies.

—Leon Trotsky, Russian
communist revolutionary

Shared pain is lessened; shared joy, increased—thus do we refute entropy.

—Spider Robinson, Canadian
science-fiction writer

Freedom does not consist in any dreamt-of independence from natural laws, but in the knowledge of these laws, and in the possibility this gives of systematically making them work towards definite ends.
—Friedrich Engels, German Marxist theorist

The problem in this world is to avoid concentration of power—we must have a dispersion of power.
—Milton Friedman, American economist

People with healthy self-esteem do not need to create pretend identities.
—bell hooks (pen name), American writer and activist

Donuts—is there anything they can't do?
—Homer Simpson, father

The usefulness of an opinion is itself matter of opinion.
>
> —John Stuart Mill, British philosopher

Where choice is set between cowardice and violence, I would advise violence.
>
> —Nelson Mandela, South African activist
> and politician, citing Gandhi

Had Mother Nature been a real parent, she would have been in jail for child abuse and murder.
>
> —Nick Bostrom, director of the
> Future of Humanity Institute

It is hardly possible to build anything if frustration, bitterness, and a mood of helplessness prevail.
>
> —Lech Walesa, Polish trade-union organizer

God gave me my money.

—John D. Rockefeller,
American industrialist

———

The basic tool for the manipulation of reality is the manipulation of words. If you can control the meaning of words, you can control the people who must use the words.

—Philip K. Dick, American
science-fiction writer

———

What a strange machine man is! You fill him with bread, wine, fish, and radishes, and out comes sighs, laughter, and dreams.

—Nikos Kazantzakis, Greek author
and philosopher

They sicken of the calm who know the storm.
—Dorothy Parker, American writer

I would have written a shorter letter, but I did not have the time.
—Blaise Pascal, French mathematician

Doubt is the origin of wisdom.
—René Descartes, French philosopher,
in *Meditations on First Philosophy*

Happiness, *n.* An agreeable sensation arising from contemplating the misery of another.
—Ambrose Bierce, American writer,
in *The Devil's Dictionary*

When we consider a book, we mustn't ask ourselves what it says but what it means.
—Umberto Eco, Italian writer,
in *The Name of the Rose*

If the world were clear, art would not exist.
—Albert Camus, French philosopher,
in *The Myth of Sisyphus*

There are no facts, only interpretations.
—Friedrich Nietzsche, German philosopher

Everyone is more or less mad on one point.
—Rudyard Kipling, British writer,
in *Plain Tales from the Hills*

Patience is a necessary ingredient of genius.
>—Benjamin Disraeli, British politician,
>in *Contarini Fleming*

I don't regard my career as something so precious
that it comes before my convictions.
>—Orson Welles, American actor
>and director

I believe there is no part of our lives, our adult as
well as child life, when we're not fantasizing, but
we prefer to relegate fantasy to children, as though
it were some tomfoolery only fit for the immature
minds of the young.
>—Maurice Sendak, American writer and
>illustrator of children's books

If they give you ruled paper, write the other way.
    —Juan Ramón Jiménez, Spanish poet

———————

No one knows how to love anybody's trouble.
    —Frank Stanford, American poet

———————

All human power is a compound of time and patience.
    —Honoré de Balzac, French novelist

———————

It is easy to be brave from a distance.
    —Aesop, Greek poet and fabulist

———————

To have great poets, there must be great audiences too.
    —Walt Whitman, American poet

Own only what you can carry with you; know language, know countries, know people. Let your memory be your travel bag.

—Aleksandr Solzhenitsyn, Russian
writer and activist

The great use of a life is to spend it for something that outlasts it.

—William James, American
philosopher and educator

Be nice to those you meet on the way up. They're the same folks you'll meet on the way down.

—Walter Winchell, American
journalist and commentator